Emily and
Carlo

Emily and Carlo

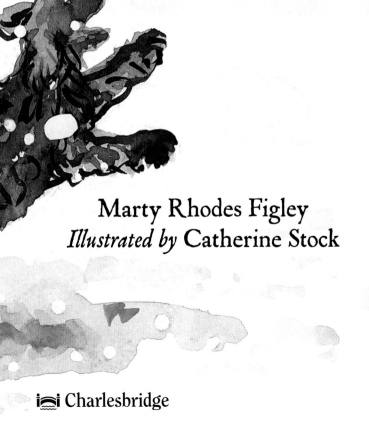

Marty Rhodes Figley

Illustrated by Catherine Stock

ini Charlesbridge

Amherst, Massachusetts, 1849

*I*n a small New England town lived a shy, smart girl named Emily.
  She loved reading and she loved writing—especially poetry.
  Home was where she was happiest.
  But the winter Emily turned nineteen, the Dickinson house
seemed empty.
  Her younger sister, Vinnie, had left for school in a different town.
  Austin, her brother, was busy at college.
  In a letter to a friend, Emily wrote:

    . . . I am all alone.

Emily's father knew she was sad.

That same winter he gave her a large, lively puppy.

When they first met, the puppy covered Emily's face with dog kisses.

She laughed.

Emily named him Carlo, after a dog in one of her favorite books.

They made a strange pair, one giant dog and one slight girl.
Emily wrote to a friend:

> *You ask of my companions, Hills, sir,*
> *and the sundown, and a dog large as myself, that my father*
> *bought me.*

With Carlo by her side, Emily had the confidence to explore the world around them.

She and Carlo walked around town, stopping every so often to visit friends.

She taught Carlo manners on these trips.

Paws were to stay on the ground—not on people's shoulders.

Sometimes Emily gave her friends lilies from her garden.

Sometimes she tucked one of her poems inside a blossom.

The beautiful flowers embarrass me,
They make me regret I am not a Bee!

To others she gave her homemade heart-shaped cakes.

Carlo loved Emily's cakes.

Most days Emily treated him to a taste.

Austin married and moved next door to Emily and Carlo's big brick house.

He and his bride named their new home the Evergreens.

Emily and Carlo walked the narrow path between the two houses.

It was *just wide enough for two who love.*

Emily and Carlo spent many happy evenings there.

A friend remembered Emily arriving at Austin's house "with her dog & Lantern. Often at the piano playing weird and beautiful melodies . . ."

Carlo played with the children.

During the day, Emily and Carlo often roamed the woods and meadows around Amherst.

Sometimes they visited the croaking frogs that lived by the pond, not far from their house.

The Frogs sing sweet today –
they have such pretty, lazy times –
how nice to be a frog!

On hot summer afternoons, Emily and Carlo stayed at home.

After chores were done, they sat on the porch, listening to the bobolinks' and robins' songs.

Emily brushed the tangles from Carlo's shaggy coat and imagined.

She wrote a poem about their make-believe trip to the ocean. It began:

I started early, took my dog,
And visited the Sea;
The mermaids in the basement
Came out to look at me,

Emily shared her hopes, her dreams—her poetry.
Carlo listened, as a good friend should.

*I talk of all these things with Carlo, and his eyes grow
meaning, and his shaggy feet keep a slower pace.*

Emily wrote:

*The Dog is the noblest work of Art . . .
his mistress's rights he doth defend —*

She called him her "shaggy ally."

In time Emily's eyes became very painful.

Twice she went away for several months to see a doctor in the city.

Carlo was left behind in Amherst.

There was no place for an old dog to stay in her boardinghouse.

Emily knew that the small, dark city room would have been awful for Carlo.

She wrote a friend:

> *Carlo did not come, because that he would die*
> *in jail . . .*

Once again, she was all alone—without her dog for company.

Emily missed Carlo, and he missed her.

Finally, Emily returned home to stay.

Carlo leaned against his best friend, decorating her clothes with dog hair.

She bent down and kissed his wet nose.

She never left him again.

As the years passed, Carlo's walk slowed.
His muzzle turned gray.
When it was time for Carlo to leave this life, it was hard to say good-bye.
Emily wrote a friend this sad, short letter:

> *Carlo died.*
>
> > *E. Dickinson*
> > *Would you instruct me now?*

Emily missed her best friend.
Carlo was her only dog for sixteen years.
She never had another.

After Carlo was gone, Emily stayed close
to home.

But the town, the woods, the meadows—
and Carlo—lived on in Emily's poetry.

'Twas my one glory—
Let it be
Remembered
I was owned of thee.

More About Emily

Emily Dickinson was born in 1830. Her father gave her Carlo sometime during the winter months of 1849–1850. Emily had returned from school at Mount Holyoke Female Seminary the year before due to illness. Named after one of the dogs in Charlotte Brontë's novel *Jane Eyre*, Carlo was probably a Newfoundland, with perhaps a little Saint Bernard mixed in.

Emily wrote many of her best poems when Carlo was alive. After she lost her walking partner, the poet, who had always been shy, became even more reclusive. She wrote, "I explore but little since my mute Confederate."

Upon Emily's death in 1886, her sister, Lavinia, discovered hundreds of poems Emily had written. They were tucked away in the bottom drawer of a cherry bureau in Emily's bedroom. We now know of almost eighteen hundred poems that Emily composed. Only ten were published in her lifetime. Today Emily Dickinson is one of our most admired poets. Her fame has spread across the world.

Author's Note

The italicized words in this manuscript are taken from Emily's poems and letters. The main events in this book are true, though some details came from my imagination. Readers must make their own decisions as to the number of dog kisses Carlo bestowed on Emily or if she really fed him her heart-shaped cakes!

When I was the same age that Emily was when she met Carlo, I met my first Newfoundland. Londerry belonged to my future husband's aunt and uncle. After Londerry's enthusiastic greeting, I was horrified to find the white dress I wore covered with dog saliva and dog hair. Newfoundlands are huge, drooling, shedding dogs. They are also handsome, friendly, brave, and loyal.

Many years later, as a Frances Perkins Scholar at Mount Holyoke College, I took a class about Emily at the Emily Dickinson Homestead in Amherst, Massachusetts. When I learned that Carlo was Emily's constant companion for sixteen years, I gained new insight about this poet. With Carlo around, her dresses probably ended up like mine had. I now saw Emily as a person who formed a long, loving relationship with a very large, messy dog.

After my Emily Dickinson class was finished, I volunteered next door at the Evergreens for a semester. When I walked down the path between the two houses, I could imagine Carlo chasing squirrels or being ordered off the porch by Emily's sister, Vinnie. He must have been a hard dog to ignore but an easy dog for Emily to love.

Sources of Quotations

Note: The sources listed are the ones consulted by the author. The additional citations from Thomas H. Johnson's *The Letters of Emily Dickinson* (Cambridge, MA: Harvard University Press, 1958) and R. W. Franklin's *The Poems of Emily Dickinson* (Cambridge, MA: Harvard University Press, 1998) are given for the reader's convenience only.

p. 5: *. . . I am all alone.* Martha Dickinson Bianchi. *Emily Dickinson Face to Face* (Boston: Houghton Mifflin, 1932), p. 193. Harvard: (L 165) Johnson

p. 9: *You ask of my companions, Hills, sir, and the sundown, and a dog large as myself, that my father bought me.* Martha Dickinson Bianchi. *The Life and Letters of Emily Dickinson.* (Boston: Houghton Mifflin, 1924), p. 239. Harvard: (L 261)

p.10:   *The beautiful flowers embarrass me,*
          They make me regret I am not a Bee!
Boston Cooking School Magazine, 11 (June–July 1906), p. 15. Harvard: (Fr 808) Franklin

p. 13: *just wide enough for two who love.* Life and Letters, p. 52.

p. 14: *with her dog & Lantern. Often at the piano playing weird and beautiful melodies . . .* Habegger, Alfred. *My Wars Are Laid Away in Books.* (New York: Random House, 2001). Emily Dickinson's friend, Kate Scott Turner, quoted on p. 373.

p. 16: *The frogs sing sweet today – they have such pretty, lazy times – how nice to be a frog!* Life and Letters, p. 232. Harvard: (L 262)

p. 18:   *I started early, took my dog,*
           And visited the sea;
           The mermaids in the basement
           Came out to look at me,
Poems of Emily Dickinson (Boston: Roberts Brothers, 1891), p. 134. Harvard: (Fr 656)

p. 20: *I talk of all these things with Carlo, and his eyes grow meaning, and his shaggy feet keep a slower pace.* Life and Letters, p. 204. Harvard: (L 212)

p. 20: *The Dog is the noblest work of Art . . . his mistress's rights he doth defend—* The Indicator (Amherst College), II, February 1850. Harvard: (L34)

p. 20: *She called him her "shaggy ally." My shaggy ally assented.* Life and Letters, p. 248. Harvard: (L280)

p. 22: *Carlo did not come, because that he would die in jail . . .* Life and Letters, p. 262. Harvard: (L 290)

p. 26:   *Carlo died.   E. Dickinson*
           Would you instruct me now?
Atlantic Monthly LXVIII, October 1891, p. 450. Harvard: (L314)

p. 28:   *'Twas my one glory—*
           Let it be
           Remembered
           I was owned of thee.
Emily Dickinson. *Bolts of Melody.* Eds. Mabel Loomis Todd and Millicent Todd Bingham. (New York: Harper Brothers, 1945), p. 168. Harvard: (F1040)

For Martha Ackmann, inspiring teacher and friend–M. R. F.
For C. S.–C. S.

Bibliography

Allen, Mary Adèle. *Around a Village Green.* Northampton, MA: The Kraushar Press, 1939.

Bianchi, Martha Dickinson. *Emily Dickinson Face to Face.* Boston: Houghton Mifflin Company, 1932.

Dickinson, Emily. *The Poems of Emily Dickinson.* Edited by R. W. Franklin. 3 vols. Cambridge, MA: Harvard University Press, 1998.

Johnson, Thomas H., and Theodora Ward, eds. *The Letters of Emily Dickinson.* 3 vols. Cambridge, MA: Harvard University Press, 1958.

Habegger, Alfred. *My Wars Are Laid Away in Books: The Life of Emily Dickinson* New York: Random House, 2001.

Leyda, Jay. *The Years and Hours of Emily Dickinson.* New Haven, CT: Yale University Press, 1960.

Text copyright © 2012 by Marty Rhodes Figley
Illustrations copyright © 2012 by Catherine Stock
All rights reserved, including the right of reproduction in whole or in part in any form.
Charlesbridge and colophon are registered trademarks of Charlesbridge Publishing, Inc.

Published by Charlesbridge
85 Main Street
Watertown, MA 02472
(617) 926-0329
www.charlesbridge.com

Library of Congress Cataloging-in-Publication Data
Figley, Marty Rhodes, 1948–
    Emily and Carlo / Marty Rhodes Figley; illustrated by Catherine Stock.
        p. cm.
    Summary: The only sibling left in the Dickinson house in Amherst, Massachusetts, in the winter of 1849, Emily gets a dog who becomes her constant companion and who is featured in some of the poems she writes. Includes brief notes on the life and work of Emily Dickinson. Includes bibliographical references.
        ISBN 978-1-58089-274-2 (reinforced for library use)
    1. Dickinson, Emily, 1830–1886—Juvenile fiction. [1. Dickinson, Emily, 1830–1886—Fiction.
    2. Poets, American—Fiction. 3. Dogs—Fiction. 4. Amherst (Mass.)—History—19th century—Fiction.]
    I. Stock, Catherine, ill. II. Title.
    PZ7.F487Emi 2012
    [E]—dc22   2011000658

Printed in China
(hc) 10 9 8 7 6 5 4 3 2 1

Illustrations done in watercolor on Arches paper
Display type and text type set in Platthand, P22 Mayflower, and Espinosa Nova
Color separations by KHL Chroma Graphics, Singapore
Printed and bound September 2011 by Jade Productions in Heyuan, Guangdong, China
Production supervision by Brian G. Walker
Designed by Susan Mallory Sherman